I ALWAYS WALK
RIGHT NEXT TO DEATH

and

Other Poems of Life

Robert Parson Crosby

Vivo! Publishing Co., Inc.
2002, 2014

To Kris and Cathay who will,
more than most,
grasp deeply the first poem,

and to Carol who was "touched by death"
on September 11, 2001,
while working at the World Trade Center.

©2002, 2014 Vivo! Publishing Co., Inc.
ISBN: 0-87810-046-6
Layout by Chris Crosby

Table of Contents

RIGHT NEXT TO DEATH

I always walk right next to death,
Just a touch away,
It may reach o'er and take my breath
And end my mortal stay.

This presence need not morbid be
Nor need it be denied,
I simply brush reality
To know it's at my side

Each moment then may be my last,
Each smile, each word, each deed
If this be so then I can cast
Away my pretense need

That I be this or I be that
And I be who I'm not,
That I be who I think you'll like,
That I be who you thought

If very moment of my life
Be this moment - no more,
Perhaps I then can choose to be
My truthful self, my core.

This death - my wise old self
My anchor in life's fray
I always walk right next to death,
Just a touch away.

THE GODS ARE GONE

The gods have fallen
The world is round
The faithful listen
There is no sound
But the ever shifting ground.

Where, oh where, may truth be found?

First, truth itself must go through fire
Be purged of the romance desire
That it be consummate and pure
False promises that reassure
This embossed version shall endure!

Then, only then, can truth be found
Ironically - on shifting ground.

The deep, deep sigh for you, for me
Comes when we quit so frantically
Chasing goblins for THE word
And find our peace in the absurd.

For truth, like standing on the sand
. . . ankle deep, twixt sea and land
Is beauty, fear, tide in, tide out
A swell of joy, a pang of doubt.

inspired by a visit to Greece in 1978

WHAT AM I LIVING FOR?

When I would be my deepest truth,
When I would be my core
I find the question turned on me -
What am I living for?

Sometimes I envy tribes of old
With all the answers clear,
The earth was flat, their roles defined,
Their gods were always near.

But where has heaven gone today
And where are all the wise
And who can find the gods to guide
And how vast are the skies?

Who speaks of those of old with faith
As if theirs was sublime,
It takes a kind of faith today
That transcends space and time.

To posit faith that there's a path
Unique where no one's tread
And take that path though where it leads
Cannot be writ or said.

LOST

There's sadness hovering over me
As fog engulfs a hushed valley,
A silence that is all its own -
A moment just to be alone.

The eerie beauty in that place
Is tempered by a somber trace
Of listless helpless come what may,
I cannot seem to find my way.

A LITTLE CORNER OF MY SOUL

There is a corner of my soul
That's tender like a fledgling foal
Where only special people dwell
And serve me water from their well.

No bumbling fool can reach me there,
Just those who give me loving care
And, more than that, who also share
Their private corner laid out bare.

How I'm thankful for those ones
Without whom I would cease to be,
For strong as I may sometimes seem
There is a fragile part of me,
A little corner of my soul
That aches for love to keep me whole.

written for Tony

Love and LOVE

Love *is* a short-lived episode
And then *it* ends - and dreams explode,
But pain and distance need not be
If LOVE has grown so tenderly
To be whatever it can be
And not to ask for fantasy.

written thinking of estranged friends
while walking up London's Drury Lane

I WANT A PARTNER

I want a partner
With whom I can dance. . .
Who joins me in the quest of life
Lived simply,
Who does not ask
Of me
Or us
Or life
Too much of what it cannot bring

AND EACH IS EVERYONE

As suddenly as I could share
Past pain and hurt with you
I'd see your eyes come open wide
And your heart breathe, "Me, too!"

Again and yet again those words
Formed on your lips and mine
Until we laughed and were amazed
At how we intertwine.

Could be in the vast scheme of life
When all is said and done
That I am you and you are me
And each is everyone.

LOVE'S FIRST FLUSH

Love's first flush apparently
Enshrines itself in mystery
A smiling glance–what majesty
To fall in love–what ecstasy.

Yet awe is ill prepared to meet
The newly loved with muddy feet!

Together by whatever dreams
The steadfast tie–or so it seems
Is choice–clear choice–to choose to care
Transending downs/lost sparks/despair

Complexities–old roles and new
Unravel–and what's shining through
Affirms that feelings I can own
But only choice deserves the throne

TO LOVE AGAIN

To love and lose yet love again
Without regard for loss or pain—
To risk oneself and naked be,
Affirming love still will remain,
To offer self so vulnerably,
To yearn and feel both hope and fear
Yet choose to clearly bet on hope
And sense a slowly forming tear
Move down my cheek
And thus announce
That caution no more has the throne,
Abandon has moved troops in here
And risk has come unto its own.

THAT WHICH I PRIZE

Lord, how I'd like to have my eyes
Be wise . . . and prize
Not an image from a glamour book
But a person with a caring look.

If I were blind I'd surely find
Your soul and heart, your core, your mind—
I wonder if I use my eyes
To keep me from that which I prize

LOVE MADE BARE

I hadn't counted it would be
That I would "fall in love" with thee,
Sharp fear engulfs each word I share
Of my attraction:
Love made bare
A fear that you will hear this word
And turn it to demand absurd
And think because of love I've shown
That now your life is less your own

A GAME?

Can. possibly, two people meet
And love each other–both–complete,
It seems it doesn't work that way,
That if I love, you go away,
Or if you care, I do not stay . . .
Maybe it's a game we play.

SO HARD TO SHARE

I have a million reasons why
My love for you should stay inside,
'Tis foolish to expose myself,
Not let my tender feelings hide.

But far more foolish to believe
That it's so hard to share;
A sadder, paralyzing pain
Is feigning "I don't care"

WE MET BUT NEVER MET

I met her and we never met—
We looked and had no sight,
Our time together seemed to pass
Like ships on foggy night.

How strange that we could be right there
A reach or so between
And yet we were a million miles
Apart—or so it seemed.

So much I wanted to be caught
In a lovers net.
That dream of dreams was not to be
We met but never met.

FACES OF LOVE

Tell me, Sage, the words of love
That I may know deep inner peace.
Beware, my child, for in your search
Emerging meanings will not cease.

Some will warm you
Make life gay
Spawning dreams like
Child at play.

Other love, more painfully
Comes disguised as enemy.

A lover true is one whose eyes
Stare at mine when I would stray
. . . and deflect simple, loving strokes
. . . by shift of thought or glance away.

Intensity seems sharp and tough
Confronting when I'd rather bluff.
Pain and fear may help me miss
That such a love is seed to bliss.

The love that feels the most absurd
Is one whose voice is rarely heard
As anything but selfish pride.
'Tis love that separates and parts,
And builds anew o'er broken hearts.

EMOTIONS

Joy and sorrow are both a part of me
Like birth and death know pain and ecstasy
They seem to dwell in awesome unity.

How often in a time alone
I gasp and cry in agony
While also I'm in ecstacy—
Not two emotions,
One it seems,
The unfulfilled and realized dreams.

TWO PAINS I KNOW ABOUT

There are two pains I know about -
With one I'm in, the other out,
The out pain's when a lover leaves
And makes it clear there's no reprieve,
My power's gone, my compass lost,
Through restless nights I count the cost.

A pain that is yet deeper still
Is when I'm in and loved so well
Yet cannot for whatever reason
Live that love in its due season.

BACCHUS

What's in a glass of wine for me,
From whence doth come its mystery
I love its color, deep and clear,
A gift tonight from yesteryear.

When this was grape upon a vine,
I wonder if it by design
Knew someday, somewhere we would meet
And make this evening more complete.

NEXT YEAR I'M FORTY-FIVE

I better kick my heels and move
And keep myself right in the groove
Cause soon I'll cease to be alive—
My God, next year I'm forty-five!

My juices then may cease to flow,
But worse than that, where'er I go
No sexy cat will look at me
And build a spicy fantasy.

I have to reassess my space,
The mirror does reflect a face
With lines and shadows not once known
But which I clearly have to own.

What really lies around the bend?
Is age a blessing in the end,
Or is there nothing else to say
Since no one can prevent that day?

for my special friend Ron Short

ABOUT BEING FIFTY

It's a time to let dreams flourish and to really "get it"
that reality is that which I create within.
It's a time to allow myself to be reborn—to love knowing
now that love is
the only way left to go . . . and in allowing myself to be
reborn to allow
others the same . . . to forgive where I asume forgiveness
is needed . . .
to sigh a deep sigh of peace and to sense order
all the while knowing that
life is . . .

    Never as peaceful
    Never as sensical
    Never as ordered
    as my illusionary
        self wishes.

And in the full knowledge of my constantly shifting
reality I shed tears of joy that I am alive and in the very
place I am at this very moment.

PROFOUND EVENTS OF LIFE

What are the profound events of life?
  a knowing glance
  a touch
  the moment when I feel
    at-one with you
  exhilaration
    shared insight
  a tear
      seen
  a tear
     received
    by me from you
    by you from me
  anger
      felt
      owned
      not turned into blame
  fear
      felt
      savored
      not denied
  warmth
      felt
      shared
      not deflected

CREATIVE MOMENTS

Creative moments are easy for me
Ideas flowing, bubbling, free
Revealing my innermost mystery.
But those in-between moments when nothing is there
And I sit pen in hand with no words to share.
A teeter–a totter goes up and comes down
And life is a balance of serious and clown.
Sometimes the wind blows and sometimes it's calm
The storm spreads the seeds and the quiet brings balm
How is it that I find it so hard to face
The quiet plateaus as they enter my space
Even that phrase (quote) "they 'enter' my space"
Like they come from outside - from some darker place
Is a clue that my quiet I've yet to embrace.

NON-SENSE

A snake said "hi" to me today
I heard the words but looked away
I couldn't imagine that the sound
Came from a snake down on the ground

Well, wouldn't you be puzzled, too
And not just know quite what to do
And never think that it could be
A snake - come on - reality!

Now some folks never will believe
The story you do now receive
They're cynical, you know the kind
They go through life and never find
The magic and the make-believe
The crazy stories poets weave

They think that life is like it looks
And miss the truth in storybooks.

VENEZIA

If there's no more to write or say
Than what's already written
Then what am I to do today
To honor how I'm smitten

By this fair city
Stone and sea
Atlantis elevated
Where romance reigns
And history rings
No matter how debated.

Vivaldi, Leonardo
And Casanova's grace
Combine to capture mystery
In every human face.

Behind the Car-ni-val-le masks
What gender, age or class
Lies deep within each human eye
As these lives swiftly pass.

For Venice now and Venice then
And Venice still to be
Transcends the life of each of us
That magic on the sea.

August 25, 2001

IN SOUTHERN FRANCE

A window in a quaint hotel,
A village in southern France,
Wooden shutters open wide
Inviting crisp, cool wind *inside.*

My window opens toward a tower
Built long ago near vintage vine.
Cars weave on ancient cobbled streets
Of stone from Britain exchanged for wine.

Nearby is a chateau named Ausone
A Roman poet in 383
It's hard for me to comprehend
There ever was 383
With New World rootlessness *in* me.

I wonder what *it* means to live
Amidst a timelessness like this.

Imagine as a little one
To know that where I live I'll die.
The cemetery I walk through
Near where the people laugh and cry
And carry out their daily fare
(maybe in my back yard at home
I'll put a small stone marker there).

I wonder what it's like to live
With death's reminder close at hand,
To read the names of family past
And see a stone reserved for me.

I do not like my rootlessness,
At least, not so today
I want to feel my roots run deep,
And have within the simple sense
Of who I am, from whence I've come
And where I'll finally rest in sleep.

OLETSA[1] ARBAT

The magic of the Arbat
Oletsal with a heart
Once graced by mighty Pushkin
Is live again with art.

To stroll its mall-like by-way
With teeming artists free
Impassioned poets orate
Away with tyranny.

What's this familiar sound I hear
Played with New Orleans skill
Jazz here on the Oletsa
A carton is the till.

St. Basel's brilliant tones
Woodwork touched with grace
Artists, easels everywhere
Moscow—a different face.

A Cafeteria here
Ovashi[2] over there
Quick join this line while I
See what this wait will buy

The Cafeteria's bleak
Ovashi there are two
The line yields fresh meat pie
A treat amidst the few.

reflections on a Moscow trip with Patricia May 1989

Always marowjinnao[3]
The tourist fare is fine
But for the Russian on the street
More waiting in a line.

Money changers, money changers
Russian roulette
"Ten rubles for a dollar, friend"
You learn to answer "Nyet."

Amidst the hope of Arbat Street
Is constant oversight
They look, they listen, will they act
With "Militzander" might?

Is this the new? Is this the old?
Both deeply stay embedded.
Do opposites, indeed, attract
Could these two soon be wedded?

My magicians of the Arbat
Are these, though there are more
Alexie, tender poet
Yuri, troubadour.

We sang and talked of life
With Yuri every day
Had chance encounters with
Alexie and Sergei

Dear Misha and kind Illich
Soldiers they had been
And Kirell and Nadja
Countless, many friends

Our focus was on Arbat
But then there was Vadim
Who thought it was his "duty"
To share his Russian dream

We saw his church at worship
The chanting and the prayers
We heard his sense of glasnost[4]
His cynical despair.

A land of stunning paradox
Where hopes are mixed with fears
The memory of the Arbat
Brings joy amidst the tears.

1. *Oletsa: street*

2. *Ovashi: vegetables*

3. *Maroujinnao: ice cream*

4. *Glasnost: openness*

IN AWE OF AGING

From the time of our conception
We all began to age.
Why do folks deny that?
Why isn't age "the rage"?

Indeed when we are young
We want to grow up quickly.
And once we're past our twenties
The question becomes prickly. . .

How old are you? My dear!
That is not for you to know.
I've spent a ton of money
for my wrinkles not to show.

But Pride of just the age I am
Affirms each day of life.
Since no one can prevent the flow
from whence comes all this strife?

Why this remorse? Why this disdain?
And why deny the truth?
Is this not hatred of what is. . .
This glorifying youth?

I, for one, affirm my age
I celebrate, I tell.
To want to be the age I'm not
Would be for me - a hell.

Move over ego on this point
You do not serve me well.
As years go by I'll be the one
Who rings the birthday bell!

VAN GOGH

There's a background to this story
That I'm about to tell
To appreciate the punch line
You need to know it well.

It seems the Van Gogh family
Was proud of its descent
And knew it would be dignified
By all but son Vincent.

His uncles owned the galleries
In Belgium, Holland, France,
Where painting drawn with proper strokes
Was sure to have its chance.

But art was not the only test
For those who were his kin
Morality must be maintained
How dare you live in sin.

And furthermore, your clothes are rags
You live on Theo's francs
You have no job, not even work
Your art is crude, no thanks.

Your countless eccentricities,
Do mortify us all
With you around, your sister's fate,
May be that no men call.

A fantasy I relish in
(Blacksheep, I too, have been)
Would be to gather all Van Goghs
Embarrassed by this kin.

In Paris first, then Amsterdam
Through Europe then the east,
To Pushkin and the Hermitage
On all this let them feast.

Then on to the Americas
The world lifts up his fame
And they will know that he they scorned,
Immortalized their name.

BY LOOKING TO THE PAST

To visit Emily Dickinson
Sip wine with Paul Cezanne
A cafe on a cobbled street
Passion, fire, elan.

To vibrate in their special space
And live my fantasy
mid rumors of the world they knew,
a moment just for me.

I'd listen with a special ear,
My eyes would watch with care,
I'd drink in every single word–
An honor to be there.

But so few went to Emily–
Cezanne, he was alone,
Suppose by looking to the past
We miss our very own!

I can walk in your living room
And have a cup of tea
Then drink in all the gift that's you
While you can feast on me.

EMILY

I read a poem by Emily
That was betwixt between
She coined a phrase at every turn
That nearly rhymed, *it* seemed.

She wrote of bees and reverie
With unexpected ease
Expanded possibility
Magnetic–if you please.

A TRIBUTE TO L.B. SHARP

What *is* the name
Of yonder tree?
It has no name but this

That *it* has bark with furrows deep
And leaves with valleys green.
Gold blossoms grace the limbs *in* spring
And roots take hold unseen

Midst myriads of teeming life
Where miracles abound
A web that's only dimly known
Yet fortifies the ground

So those who ask "what is the name?"
Can breathe and drink and live!
To KNOW the tree—caress the trunk,
The leaf, the soil, and give

But passing fancy to the words
Assigned *in* this great game
Lest we forget that all of life
Is deeper than its name!

SOREN KIERKEGARD

The truth consists
   not in
   knowing
    the
   truth
   but in
      being
The truth.

Being consists
   not of any definition
   but of
      BEING!
    Simply Being . . .
     Here
     Now.

SALVATION

Salvation
. . . is not a future event
    is not something you can think yourself into
    is not a one-time only event
    is not accompanied with any dogma
    is not exclusive to any one religion
    or even to religion itself.
    is not to save you from a bad future consequence.

Salvation
. . . is about feeling cleansed right here, right now, for now.
. . . is foreign to your mind's insistence on continual bitterness or continual regret about the past or endless repetitive worry about the future.

Salvation
. . . is to be grasped now without further thinking. It's as simple to say yes to as it would be to drop a hot coal from your hands.

Huang-Po[1] says,
"Ordinary beings are the Buddha, just as they are."
    Take a deep breath
    Slowly leave it out
    Realize your Buddha within, your divinity,
    your oneness with the universe.
    Just as you are.
    . . . now!

inspired, in part, by reading Eckhart Tolle

[1] 9th Century

39

I WAS NOT MYSELF TODAY

"I was not myself today."
What a strange and curious thing to say.
Are there two me's? One false? One true?
How can I know which one comes through?

Who is this "I" who lets me down,
Or, is it the other way around?
Is it myself who easily slides,
For self-protection, to those places
Where I and myself wear different faces.

What is this that "I" call "myself"
Except an essence flashing bye
Of love, compassion, joy that springs
From deep within and ne'er runs dry,

And yet a well from which, at times
I do not draw—thus lose myself.
I want the "I" that others see
To be "my self" who lives in me.

ON THE SUDDEN DEATH OF A FRIEND

Death seems so abrupt.
It does not kindly knock, but interrupts
And grants no further talk.

Thoughts that flowed will be no more,
Death has come and shut the door.

Our dialogue now is in my head.
I imagine what you might have said.

What mystery lies beyond the tomb?
Is death, again another womb
Or is it done for you and me,

No future life or mystery?

THE ETERNAL NOW

I have lived in very bleak circumstances. The streets of my city were made of gold. Choirs sang cherubic music all day - all night. Nobody aged. My mother remained 23 all of her life. By request I became 25 - forever. All my needs were granted. There was no illness. My bones never ached.

Nobody cried. No tears were shed at parting for we knew that we would never part. No sorrow. No anger. I loved that life. I don't know for how long, time was not measured there. Then I slowly began to experience what you mortals call - boredom.

The first time I felt it - boredom - a voice spoke to me as if from a giant loudspeaker. "Robert, discipline yourself. This is a place of great joy. Do not dwell on joyless feelings."

Somebody knew my unspoken thoughts!

The feeling increased and I soon was instructed to stop at a discipline care center. I hadn't noticed that there was one on every corner.

They gave me a small tablet, in a gold wrapper. "One a day" they said, these lovely winged creatures.

I don't know how, but I escaped. Perhaps a bad pill. It seems that someone succeeded in circulating an Orwellian like book and I got it that this eternal bliss place was not for me. But the alternatives were bleak. Since we were immortal, suicide was not an option. A small group of us met (without detection, we thought) and dreamed of another life where:

. . . Seeds grew and died
. . . People aged
. . . All things ended
. . . Everyone knew that each moment was
    transient and, therefore, precious
. . . Cities weren't golden but were what we
    created them to be
. . . People cried and laughed, hated
    and loved.
. . . There was pain, suffering and unwanted
    killing.
. . . We would be the creators of our
    own lives!
But we were detected. Our punishment was to be sent to
this "heaven" of our
fantasy - planet Earth. And every moment I am here
        I realize more and more
            that to be
                fully present
            now
                is
    the immortality I dreamed of.
    There is no further shore.

Inhaling each precious moment knowing that it is
transient, and walking on dirt, grass, and sidewalks, sure
beats walking on gold.

Occasionally, by mistake, I turn my car radio dial to a
station as a voice is saying "Are you ready for the streets
of gold . . ." and "He knows your every thought."

I shudder!

The little critic inside me
Chuckles at my poetry
And then assumes that
So do thee.

CPSIA information can be obtained at www.ICGtesting.com
Printed in the USA
BVOW01s1550170315

392056BV00006B/60/P